Can You Love Me With My Scars

James G. Savoy

Copyright © 2024 James G. Savoy

All Rights Reserved

Dedication

I dedicate this book to all those who are reading it and who have dealt with some level of scars. This is for those who have suffered with hidden wounds that nobody could see. This book is for the victims who turned into survivors.

I dedicate this book to those who have been tasked with the responsibility of loving someone dealing with scars. I know it's not easy to deal with a scarred generation because as you prepare to take this journey in this reading, you will find out that it is therapeutic, enlightening, and transformative in its own sense.

I dedicate this book to all my readers out there.

Thank you for trusting me with your time because I know that is valuable and every minute should be maximized.

Acknowledgment

I want to first take the time to recognize, honor, and acknowledge God gave me the confidence and wisdom to take real-life experiences and turn them into ministry tools.

I want to acknowledge my mentors and all those spiritual leaders who have at some time or another played a significant role in my life.

I wrote this book at a very challenging season of my life. This book was written during a time when I was diagnosed with Pulmonary Sarcoidosis, which is a disease that severely attacked my immune system and my lungs, leaving me breathing, fatigued, and weight loss. God placed some very special people and strong supporters in my corner to help me through this difficult time. To Pastor Ronald and Toni George, Pastor R.C and Lady Calligan, Bishop James and Sheila Gardiner, Pastor Ray and Minister Kim Bell, Pastor Demetrius and Lady Adrienna Wilson, Elder Diggs, Pastor Charlie, and Pamela Smith, to my childhood and adult best friend Elmer Lowe for always giving me a listening ear anytime I needed it and to Momma Beth Lowe, it was your love me years ago that saved my life, and for that, I say thank you and last but not least my spiritual father as well as mentor, Arch-Bishop Carl Mccomb. I couldn't have made it without you all. I acknowledge everyone who sent offers of prayers for me. With much prayer and a strong support system, by the grace of almighty God, the book is now here.

CONTENTS

Dedication iii

Acknowledgment iv

Foreword vi

Chapter 1 – The Idea Of What Love Is 1

Chapter 2 – Knowing Love from God's Perspective 7

Chapter 3 – The Proper Examination Of Scars 17

Chapter 4 – Traumas, Triggers, & Testimonies 25

Chapter 5 – Do You Have The Capacity To Love Me Through This 32

Chapter 6 – Dealing With A Wounded Spirit 37

Chapter 7 – Unveiling The Root Of Bitterness 46

Chapter 8 – I Forgive You, But I'm Still Offended 52

Chapter 9 – I Trusted You With My Heart 63

Chapter 10 – I'm Waiting on My Physician 69

Chapter 11 – The Benediction: A Word for The Scarred 75

About the Author 76

Foreword

By: Pastor Demetrius Wilson

The Apostle Paul pinned some of the most prolific points concerning the reality of love in 1st. Corinthians 15. In verse 7, we read that it believes, hopes, and endures all things. As the chapter ends, he denotes three great things, with love being the greatest of them all. It is something that cannot be fully explained. The very existence of genuine love is supernatural. It is more than emotion and far beyond what the human heart can produce. It is only found in the sovereign nature of our creator, YAHWEH. John penned a most definitive statement that declares that the Father is love.

My friend and brother have issued a challenge through the words of this book, asking the question as to whether we would choose to embrace the experience that causes us to demonstrate the ability to see beyond the appearance of that which is unattractive... the scars! Is possible that love will help us to realize that the evidence of a past, does not supersede purpose?

I pray that you will find the words of the preceding pages insightful and thought-provoking. May we make the quality choice in love!

- Shalom

Chapter 1 – The Idea Of What Love Is

As we attempt to understand the concept of the word love, we sometimes will struggle, because let the truth be told we view love from a place of broken mechanics which is the heart.

Jeremiah 17:9 states, *"The heart is deceitful above all things and desperately wicked: who can know it?"*

This emphasizes that the human heart is fundamentally deceitful and wicked and cannot be trusted because it's like viewing the world through a shattered glass mirror.

So, as we look at the idea of what love is, let's embrace logic, facts, and Biblical insights into the very idea of what love is. We hear it every day: people will say or use the word so commonly that we rob it of its value because we enmeshed it as a part of our casual conversation. Why do some people use the word love too much in every sentence they speak while talking with others? (Not necessarily close friends). Is this habit normal? It's like our closing remarks to every conversation.

Using the word love frequently or in every sentence can indicate an overuse of the word, which might not necessarily reflect its authenticity of. People use it as an expression of affection, to make the conversation more lighthearted and worthy. However, it can also be seen as insincere or ineffective in its purpose and true nature.

Webster says love is a quality or feeling of strong or constant affection for and dedication to another. So when we connect the dots and attempt to connect the definition to the casualty of conversation, the two simply don't connect.

Love Is the Foundation

In any type of relationship love is the key ingredient and if we are talking about the foundation of a relationship, love gives it the grace to grow in consisted of ways. Growing into your knowledge of the foundations of love is imperative to living the Kingdom the life that God intended.

An effective, solid foundation for love typically involves several key elements and aspects that help nurture and sustain a healthy and fulfilling relationship. Here are some important components that can contribute to a

A solid foundation for love:

1. *Trust:* Trust is essential in any type of relationship. All parties involved should be able to rely on each other, be honest, and have faith in the accountability process.

2. ***Communication:*** Open and honest communication is crucial for maintaining a solid foundation for love.

3. ***Respect:*** Mutual respect is vital in a relationship. We should value each other's opinions, boundaries, and individuality and always execute the power of consideration.

4. ***Support:*** Being there for each other through thick and thin is important for building a solid foundation for love.

5. ***Shared values and goals:*** Having common values, beliefs, and goals can strengthen the bond between partners. When both individuals are aligned in their vision for the future, it can create a sense of unity and purpose in the relationship.

6. ***Quality time together:*** Spending quality time together, engaging in activities that both partners enjoy, and making time for each other amidst busy schedules can help nurture love and deepen the connection.

7. ***Empathy and understanding:*** Showing empathy, understanding, and compassion towards each other's feelings and experiences can foster a deeper emotional connection and strengthen the bond between partners.

8. ***Compromise and flexibility:*** Being willing to compromise, negotiate, and adapt to each other's needs and preferences is important for resolving conflicts and maintaining harmony in the relationship.

9. ***Commitment:*** A solid foundation for love requires a commitment from both partners to prioritize the relationship, work through challenges together, and invest time and effort into nurturing their connection.

Now that we know that love is the foundation and have somewhat of an understanding of the term, it challenges us to address the elephant in the room and through observation draw the hard truth or conclusion that do we really know what love is. Many of us are challenged to define love, and even those of us who can define it often find that others may not agree with our insight on the topic, yet we all have an idea of what love is.

There is a whole cultural phenomenon and industry that has grown up around a misconception of love. One of the reasons is love was not modeled to us in the right way. Children are learners through observation, so with that being said, part of the issue may be somebody showed us a tainted picture of love, like two partners living in a contentious house atmosphere full of bitterness, hurt, and regret, but at the end of the day the child hears them say to each other "baby I love you."

Love is something you radiate. While radiating, love connects to everyone you encounter. You give it away without limits. However, understand that when I choose to love someone, I am taking a risk because oftentimes, it's an investment that you must be willing to release.

Understand that we expect fruitful returns, but sometimes we will experience a blank or empty investment. Loving another on the condition they love you back is a risk that you take. Love is necessarily unconditional. Conditional "love" is only by approval only. It can be negotiated and renegotiated.

Everything about world culture tries to induce us to fear, to hate, to increase friction and hostility, to be impatient, to be frustrated, or to be outraged. These things take us away from love in the opposite direction. It is our duty as believers to revisit the nature, purpose, and power of love.

As we raise our awareness and frequency of the idea of what love is we must embrace the fact that love is hard to maintain. As we raise our awareness and challenge our personal growth on the matter, love can be sustained in order to advance the kingdom we must be intentional.

Love is in your genetics and true nature. It's one of the many reasons God created you. The journey to love is the purpose of this life. Love heals you, the people around you, and the world. Reach and accept your responsibility and choose to love.

This book, in its design, has the sole purpose of com compelling us to take a closer look at our love walk. Loving people with scars is not always easy, as we will find out as we transition on this journey together. I took this approach writing this book because if God has created, called, and chosen us to love, we have to deal with the reality that we can all be guilty of having an idea of love without knowing what love really is. What better way to define love than from the purest and most effective place? That is called LIFE and all its experiences.

Can you be in love with an idea of love?

To love the idea of someone means to have strong feelings of affection, admiration, or even infatuation towards a person based on a specific image or concept of them rather than their true self or actual qualities.

Why is love not a feeling but a choice?

Why is love a choice? Love is a choice and a decision because your actions determine if it lives on or ends. You are in control of how you act in your relationships and how much you push past tests and trials. When you decide to work on communication, trust, intimacy, or emotional security, you're choosing love.

As we embark upon this journey together we are going to unlock some truths about this love walk that God has called us into. We are going to be challenged in a lot of areas of our personal life. Alright, we had an interesting icebreaker now let us go onto chapter two and see what God has to say about this issue.

Chapter 2 – Knowing Love from God's Perspective

According to the scriptures, God's love is unconditional, infinite, steadfast and inexhaustible. He loves us regardless of our worthiness or actions. He loves us because it is who he is. It is central to his character, which does not change. This type of love cannot be measured as human love. God's love is humble, not boastful or proud. It does not envy others, and it honors and respects everyone. God is so impressive that he does not present to us a Love without accountability because he chastens those whom he loves. It is very key that we understand God's love, for it's the only way we can love people who have scars in their lives. The Love of God can conquer and bring you through anything. My life principle is that if you work the principles, you will see the fruit.

"God Created Us for Fellowship"

The word fellowship is derived from the Greek word koinonia.

Koinonia can be defined as "holding something in common."

Everything that God created has a purpose. Before man was created, God already had a plan and a purpose for man. If you notice in the beginning God created the heavens and earth. To give you a deeper insight, here is an effective breakdown.

Genesis 1:1-5

"God spirit moves over formless earth and creates darkness and light and gives it a name according to verse number five, calling the light day and darkness he called night."

Genesis 1:6-8

"God creates barriers in the earth where the waters could not overlap the dry land these barriers or restrictions are called the firmament and the heavens was established."

Genesis 1:9-13

"God now gives the dry land and waters a name by calling the dry land earth and the waters he called seas and following he creates vegetation."

Genesis 1:14-19

"God creates the greater and the lesser to establish times and seasons."

Genesis 1:20-23

"God, with his spoken word, becomes Rhema as he speaks and populates the seas and the heavens."

Genesis 1:24-31

"God speaks and creates the living creatures of the field and creates man in his own image and likeness."

So now, as we look back at the breakdown of the creation, God's purpose was clear: everything that he created had to connect with one another. God's intention for mankind is made known throughout the scriptures in its entirety, but in the creation, we embrace a deeper insight. If man was to be created in the image and likeness of God, this meant that of all of God's creation, man is special and is to have a certain relationship and communion with God more than any other creature. It is obvious that man is the highlight of God's creation.

"In the redemptive work for man, Jesus dealt with sin and death [and ultimately the devil] and has given us eternal life" (Hebrews 2:14). All men can now fellowship in the life of God – as many as believe can have this fellowship and enter into the family of God, check this out!

1: Corinthians 1:9 says:

> ***"God is faithful, by whom ye were called unto the fellowship of his Son Jesus Christ our Lord."***

So now it is impossible for us to have fellowship with the Son, and if we are all believers, we must have fellowship with one another, and that is when we are introduced and exposed unto one another's SCARS. John 13:35 states it best when it declares to us that Jesus said: By this shall all men know that ye are my disciples if ye have love one to another.

In Christ Jesus, all men have the liberty to fellowship with God. Fellowship with the Son is fellowship with God. The message of the gospel is about God reconciling all men to Himself to have fellowship with man. In your walk with God, you are further educated on all that pertains to this life that you have received, as well as have knowledge on how to fellowship with one another.

As we gain more knowledge and grow in our relationship with God, it is seen in our living and conduct in the light, as well as in how we interact with unbelievers and fellow believers. You are to love one another, edify one another, forgive one another, comfort one another, and exhort one another. All these effective and accountable spiritual gut checks are the responsibility of this fellowship union.

It is from your fellowship with God that you have fellowship with other believers.

Do You Have the Capacity to Love Broken Believers?

Galatians 6:1 – *"Brethren, if a man be <u>overtaken</u> in a <u>fault,</u> ye which are spiritual, <u>restore</u> such a one in the spirit of meekness: considering thyself, lest thou also be tempted. 2: <u>Bear ye one another's burdens</u> and so fulfill the law of Christ."*

The word restore means "to strengthen and to heal through a gradual process." It reveals the idea of a broken limb (hand or leg) being strengthened requiring a stern but gentle approach to preventing the broken limb from growing out of form.

Such kind of strengthening requires hands that are firm and, at the same time, very gentle. Otherwise, the broken limb might go out of shape or be totally lost (condemned and amputated).

Here Is the Issue

The issue is never God loving us, but the issue is the creation that God has called to co-exist together has failed again and again with learning how to deal, treat, and love one another. This a true statement that can be tested in the present reality that organizations crumble because of this, Churches split or dry out because of this, and the divorce rate is rapidly climbing because we have failed to perfect this love walk that God has called us to walk in. Now I know what you are saying: everybody's situation is different, and you are so right in a sense, but however at some point, we have to put principles into practice and allow growth to take place in our love walk.

Now from God's perspective, he expects us to walk in love with one another. The concept of walking in love is a Kingdom concept that refers to living a life of love and following Christ's example. Acknowledging God's love is maintaining a close relationship with him and practicing forgiveness, holding your tongue, and not being offended which we will address in a later chapter of the book.

The Greek word translated as "love" in this passage is agape. Agape is sacrificial, unselfish, unconditional love that proves itself through actions. It perfectly describes God's love for us. With agape, *"God showed how much he loved us by sending his one and only Son into the world so that we might have eternal life through him."* When the Bible says, *"God is love"* in 1 John 4:8, the word "love" is a translation of agape. God's nature, His essence, is selfless, sacrificial, and unconditional love. In its purest form, this is love according to God.

So now, since God loves us sacrificially and unconditionally, we ought to love one another. *"Dear friends, since God so loved us, we also ought to love one another"* (1: John 4:11). *"There is no greater love than to lay down one's life for one's friends"* (John 15:13).

In first. Corinthians the 13th chapter, often referred to as the love chapter gives us an unbelievably detailed description of how to walk in love:

"Love is patient and kind. Love is not jealous, boastful, proud, or rude. It does not demand its own way. It is not irritable, and it keeps no record of wrong. It does not rejoice about injustice but rejoices whenever the truth wins out. Love never gives up, never loses faith, is always hopeful, and endures through every circumstance"

(1: Corinthians 13:4–7, N.L.T.)

In context, love is also about giving according to God's perspective because God loved the world so much that he gave his only begotten Son. When we look at love in the giving aspect, it is about releasing oneself for a greater cause. Giving ourselves up means offering our lives to God in sacrifice. It means following, obeying, submitting, serving, and living in a committed relationship with Him. Giving ourselves up means walking in love.

How Does God See Me

Second Corinthians 5:17 says, *"Therefore if anyone is in Christ, he is a new creation. The old has passed away: behold, the new has come."* When we come to Jesus for salvation, we are made completely new. We are said to be "in" Christ. We are reconciled with God and counted as righteous before Him (2: Corinthians 5:17–21). Rather than seeing our sinfulness, God sees the righteousness of His Son. He does not hold our sins against us, but having justified us, He invites us into an active relationship with Him. He sees us as people who have been redeemed and as so much more.

Oftentimes people who struggle with condemnation based on past experiences have a tough time realizing how God really sees them. Through my walk with God, I have come to know this truth, is that the God that was modeled to me is not the God that I come to know for myself. God sees me like nobody can see me, he knows me inside out.

First John 4:18 says that *"perfect love drives out fear"*. The acronym we use for fear is F.E.A.R: False evidence appearing to be real. The biblical understanding of fear should be recognized as Godly reverence. There is a fear that condemns and imprisons us in our own minds to believe that God sees us according to the naysayers.

The canceling out of the fear of condemnation is one of the main functions of God's love. The person without

Christ is under judgment and has plenty to fear (John 3:18), but once a person is in Christ, the fear of judgment is gone.

"God did not send his Son into the world to condemn the world, but in order that the world might be saved through him"

(John 3:17).

The Bible says that nothing can separate the believer from the love of God in Christ.

(Romans 8:38–39).

Romans 8:38-39 KJV

"38: For I am persuaded, that neither death, nor life, nor angels, nor principalities, nor powers, nor things present, nor things to come, 39: Nor height, nor depth, nor any other creature, shall be able to separate us from the love of God, which is in Christ Jesus our Lord."

In Summary

In our closing remarks on chapter 2, we come to understand that the love of God is what holds it all together. We have put together two perspectives or views on love. We discussed in the 1st chapter of having an idea of what is and now we have tapped into Gods perspective on love and what he expects from his children. We get ready to ride deeper into this journey of embracing the responsibility of loving people with scars.

Chapter 3 – The Proper Examination Of Scars

Everyone has a battle scar of some kind. Some are visible on the outside of our physical body, while some are hidden internally.

Webster states that a scar is a mark left on the skin or within body tissue where a wound, burn, or sore has not healed completely.

As we investigate our society, we see people every day moving in transition on their way somewhere. You view the coffee shops, and you view people in conversation talking about life, laughing out loud, but the reality is every time you encounter people, you must understand you are dealing with people with scars. <u>Some have scars that are on them, while others are dealing with scars that are in them</u>. Believe it or not, those internal soul wounds are deadly. While you are at work or in the marketplace, be conscious that the people around you might have scars. When you stand at the altar to say I do, and you are getting ready to spend the rest of your life with that soulmate, know this: they might be smiling on the outside, but later on, it is inevitable that you will be exposed to their scars. What happens when the unexpected hits your address and tragedy leaves you partially marred or scarred up to a point where you develop deep insecurities about yourself? Living with physical or spiritual scars will take faith, trust, & patience, and, most of all, being consistent with yourself.

To love a person who are living with scars you got to know what scars really are. The evidence that I been through something, and I have been left with a mark that reminds me everyday of what happened. Truthfully, this book was birthed through a real-life experience.

A young man saved and on fire for the Lord, preaching, teaching, and walking in God's power, is going forth in ministry, doing outreach, and heeding the call of God on his life. However, he felt something was missing in his life, and that missing piece was a wife with whom to grow in grace. He meets a young lady, and they connect. In his bones, he feels that they are so compatible that after dating for a few months, they are at the altar exchanging vows. Remember that when you connect with people, you just might, if you walk with them long enough, get exposed to their scars, and they may get exposed to yours.

"Being Exposed to The Scars of The One You Love"

Shortly after matrimony, he started to notice a change in her behavior, and he started to become suspicious: now, keep in mind they both have similar backgrounds of dealing with street life, and both have lived a life of addiction. So, finally, her addiction surfaces, and now he is faced with the dilemma of whether I should leave or stay. At this moment, he's trying to grow a church, and he feels that his ministry is getting ready to take off. Unfortunately, there is a ministry at home he has to deal with first. So, moving along, one day, they got into a heated argument concerning the addiction, and she looked at him with hurt, distrust, pain, and disappointment and said to him okay, now you know my flaws, but one thing I am going to tell you is this.

I am waiting for my deliverer to show up. I don't know when it will happen, but it will, but the question is, will you be patient with me in my process, or will you leave? Afterwards she went to bed.

An all-night fight with the Boogyman

All night long, he is battling in his thoughts to come up with some sense of justification to leave because he is so torn between the Love of his wife and the church community. He knows that he loves her so much, and he's up fighting with the Boogyman in his mind going round after round and seems like he's losing when really he's winning because God has allowed this Boogyman, which is the torment of his thoughts wrestle him down psychologically until he became weary, delirious, exhausted and tired and he fell on the couch in the living room area and that's when it happened. The spirit of the living God breathed on him like a strong wind, but he spoke in a small, still voice and said Son, what is troubling you in the night season? He replied to God I don't know what to do with this woman and God said to him, the truth of the matter is she has scars in her life, but I knew she had scars before she married you, so you are responsible for loving your wife. That is the oath that you took before me, and all that was present at your holy matrimony. Now she has scars, but the question is, can you learn to love her with the scars? Secondly, he says that when you learn to love her with her scars, you will find yourself developing a love that sees God's purpose over a temporary condition.

Lastly, God speaks of the love of God and how he sees flaws in his children is different from how humanity looks at their flaws, and God in his infinite wisdom leaves him paralyzed with this last statement by saying, it will benefit you to do this because one day who knows when your SCARS will show up.

He makes the decision to stay and honor the covenant so that God keeps his promise. He brought them through the process after much prayer and counseling and being intentional with this love walk, which was not easy, but God's word in (Jeremiah 30:17) speaks:

> *"I will give you back your health and heal your wounds,' says the LORD."*

Time is moving forward, and the ministry is growing by leaps and bounds. He is growing so much that they birthed out a second and third church location, and he is traveling across the states preaching and teaching God the truth. No doubt there are times when he is exhausted and tired, but as long as God gives him strength and grace, he keeps on pushing himself to do more to the point he starts to stretch himself thin and take on great assignments that he has little time to do it in, but his zeal won't let him slow down until one day.

The Boogy Man Is Back

Now, this preacher, teacher, and husband are about to face God's grace head-on when he finds himself tangled up and twisted and addicted to the unclean, lustful sin of pornography.

Yes, he has now been entangled for quite some time, and he has suppressed it, fasted over it, repented about it, and now the boogie man of the mind is back to torment him. At first, he tried his best to hold it secret and believed that some sense of private deliverance would take place, but it never happened. This boogyman was more aggressive in his thoughts and tormented him day and night. He wasn't getting any sleep, and a spirit of fear gripped him to the point that he thought that God was getting ready to send him to hell.

This was an ongoing thing of torment in the mind to the point that he thought of checking into a mental institution: this is how bad it got for him, and in the midst of it all, God, in his grace, saw fit to breathe on him again, but this time while in bed in a knot holding his head to drown out the noise in the mind he heard a preacher on T.V. speaking the scripture he heard was

<u>James 5:13-16</u>

"13: Is any among you afflicted? Let him pray. Is any merry? Let him sing psalms.

14: Is any sick among you? Let him call for the elders of the church, and let them pray over him, anointing him with oil in the name of the Lord:

15: And the prayer of faith shall save the sick, and the Lord shall raise him up: and if he has committed sins, they shall be forgiven him.

16: Confess your faults one to another, and pray one for another, that ye may be healed. The effectual fervent prayer of a righteous man availed much."

So, he at this point there was only one way out of this, and it is called CONFESSION. He sat her down and told her all about it and gracefully she looked at him and said I knew something was troubling you for your behaviors and patterns had changed and after consulting with her they decided to have a meeting with his leadership and they supported his decision to take a sabbatical and ironically her support in his process was different.

She never looked at him through a judgmental lens: in fact, she understood that addiction is addiction, and these addictions leave emotional soul scars in our lives. I told you earlier <u>some people have scars on them while others have scars in them</u>. She drove him to prayer meetings across two states to meet with Intercessory Prayer groups. This covenant wife of his was very empathetic towards his condition while still being stern by telling him I'm going to stay with you through this, but I will not compete with these images. That accountability is what he needed. She went to counseling session after a counseling session with him to take a therapeutic approach towards deliverance. They made it through this process by the grace of God, and he came back stronger in his passion for God like never before. We all have scars, but we have to be willing to process them through God's grace and his love.

Through the course of studying spiritual scars, I must admit that my views on this topic have shifted because scars signify we were in a battle. Our scars signify we were in a battle, and it reveals a wound that has been healed. The scars that we obtain as we push through life and its swift transitions keeps us grounded and humble. I stand on this: battles that are won are battles that are fought.

Scars Are Reminders

My scars remind me that it's not about but much bigger than me,

My scars remind me that you have to be chosen to carry something great,

My scars within me remind me that I have to win the battle within me before it can manifest outside me,

My scars remind me that standing power can only be birthed through pain,

My scars remind me that there was a wound connected to the scar, BUT GOD let me live to tell the story.

JAMES 1:12

"Blessed is the one who perseveres under trial because, having stood the test, that person will receive the crown of life that the Lord has promised to those who love him."

I got the scars, but I'm still here!

Chapter 4 – Traumas, Triggers, & Testimonies

In my lifetime, I have had my share of uncomfortable experiences. I grew up in a neighborhood where that consisted of gang violence, drug infestation, and chaos, yet there was unity and family knitting between my peers. There are experiences that we go through that will leave us going through trauma.

What is trauma?

A deeply distressing or disturbing experience:

"We cannot continue to address what we don't understand."

Understanding trauma involves recognizing the following:

It results from something that happened to me that I don't have the capacity to digest what just happened.

Trauma impacts you mentally, emotionally, and physically.

Avoiding trauma behaviors, for the trauma that's not addressed, doesn't leave us. It actually grows with us until we tackle it head-on.

"I quote! If you don't deal with your trauma, your trauma will one day deal with you."

When we notice unusual behavior patterns in a person in their adulthood, we sometimes scratch our heads, wondering why they continue to go through these same hurtful patterns as if they embrace them. In our mindset, we ask why you do what you whenever or however you do it. What we are fruits to a tree that is not productive. Yes, it's the visible evidence on the ground surface that we view, analyze, and judge. But here is the kicker: before we judge the behaviors by the fruit, we must discern the seed.

Matthew 7:15-20

You Will Know Them by Their Fruits

"18: A good tree cannot bear bad fruit, nor can a bad tree bear good fruit. 19: Every tree that does not bear good fruit is cut down and thrown into the fire. 20: Therefore, by their fruits, you will know them."

The seed represents the origin or the beginning stage of a thing.

The fruit is the offspring or extension of the seed.

Now, let's put it all together. The life experiences or the bad situations that happened create trauma, and trauma, which is the seed, extends from childhood through puberty to adulthood, which produces what I call trauma fruit. Here is a true saying: "traumatized people, traumatize people." It is possible that you may have experienced hurt from a person who never overcame their trauma, and now they introduce you to their fruit, and if you don't get healed from your trauma, you will be the partaker of the generational pattern that lives in the lineage until it is checked at the front door.

Established by <u>The American Psychological Association, it defines</u> trauma as an emotional response to a stressful event. After a trauma, people experience feelings of shock and denial. Long-term effects of trauma may include <u>intense emotions</u>, <u>physical symptoms</u>, <u>flashbacks</u>, and, watch this last one - <u>problems with relationships</u>.

<u>Lord, how do you deal with the traumatized?</u>

Partner with me in my process without limitations.

Be patient with me, for I am still trying to process something that is hard to make sense of.

Whatever you do, don't allow me to isolate myself from your love, counsel, and accountability.

Through my observation of scripture, David is a perfect example of the traumatized, and he writes in Psalm 34:18,

"The Lord is close to the brokenhearted and saves those who are crushed in spirit."

The term brokenhearted means *"to be shattered into pieces."*

Traumatized people put up walls around their heart

They pry on sheltering themselves from what we call the triggers of life.

Avoiding trauma triggers

What Are Triggers, and How Do They Form?

Triggers are sensual reminders that cause uncomfortable psychological rehearsals of the mind.

Triggers cause us to relive a thing over again.

A trigger can be something that activates my symptoms again.

Oftentimes, we may be going through a situation, and the triggers will recreate the atmosphere that you fought hard to get out of, and you find yourself reliving the pain again. We must constantly tell ourselves that trauma will not be our reality.

Listen, anything or anyone who convinced me that they are a trigger to my trauma! The solution is clear: I must disconnect myself from any trigger that connects me to my trauma. So the hard question to ask is: <u>are you my trigger or my solution</u>? It is very vital that you figure this out moving forward in overcoming trauma because my PEACE is expensive, and I place great value on it.

Trauma is an enemy of peace. It is safe for me to conclude that trauma is a thief and a robber, and I don't want to deal any longer with Traumas and Triggers. The understanding of the matter is that one represents a painful experience, and the other represents a reminder of the painful experience.

Now, previously, we discussed the young man and wife in there with their own personal addictions while in their marriage. Now comes the testimony, and please remember that testimony is about revealing the truth and owning it so that you can experience a real, authentic breakthrough.

In their marriage, his wife would occasionally go back and fall into her addiction, but this behavior was just the fruit: let us take a look at the seed of this thing. As we unveil the truth, you are either a <u>trigger</u> or the <u>solution</u> or answer to the problem. Let the truth be told: this husband created problems that didn't have to do with dealing with the inconsistency of his decision-making. He was very unstable. He would create bills that they didn't need, take out financial loans in secret, and lie and hide. He tried his best to conceal the matter until it was resolved, and when exposure would happen, he would create an argument to avoid healthy confrontation, and my friends that put them in a stressful situation.

Remember, trauma is the response to a stressful event, so he was being a strong contributor of stress in this situation. He helped produce an atmosphere in the house that was not conducive to a fruitful environment so in essence in that season of their marriage the man definitely was her TRIGGER and not a SOLUTION.

The stress of not having a financial security was real and the reality of it all is that why create problems where there is no problem. Stop being triggers to people who are barely surviving trauma and be the solution. Declare that I will be the balance and the peace that's needed in the house, in the church, in my organization and in my relationship.

In our conclusion of this chapter, I leave you with this,

The power of a testimony

John 9: 18-25

"18: But the Jews did not believe concerning him, that he had been blind, and received his sight until they called the parents of him that had received his sight.

19: And they asked them, saying, Is this your son, who ye say was born blind? How then doth he now see?

20: His parents answered them and said, we know that this is our son and that he was born blind:

21: But by what means he now seethe, we know not: or who hath opened his eyes, we know not: he is of age: ask him: he shall speak for himself.

22: These words spoke to his parents because they feared the Jews, for the Jews had agreed already that if any man did confess that he was Christ, he should be put out of the synagogue.

23: Therefore, said his parents, He is of age: ask him.

24: Then again called they the man that was blind, and said unto him, Give God the praise: we know that this man is a sinner.

25: He answered and said, <u>whether he be a sinner or no, I know not: one thing I know, that, whereas I was blind, now I see</u>."

Chapter 5 – Do You Have The Capacity To Love Me Through This

1: Thessalonians 3:12

"May the Lord make your love increase and overflow for each other and for everyone else, just as ours does for you."

Understanding this present truth, my friends is that people go through experiences that develop scars in their life and can sometimes cause a person to get bitter before they get better, and once you are in some type of relationship with them, you come to realize that this experience has made them difficult to love and in your thought process there is the birthing of the question, and that is do I really have the capacity to love them through whatever they are going through? In other words, you say you love me, but can you handle me and my baggage?

When you are dealing with scarred people, you have to constantly submit yourself to the counsel of the Holy Spirit guiding you on how to love them and what is needed to be effective because I believe that once you are exposed to their scars, you are now responsible for loving them through their process. One of the main things that we gotta recognize is:

Do You Understand My Pain

If you listen to the scarred with your spiritual ears, you would hear them saying to you, don't you see I'm in pain right now, and I'm struggling to get over it, and I really need your assistance?

One key insight to process is that hurt people hurts people. To understand my pain you must practice empathy with me. When someone is difficult to deal with, try to understand that they are dealing with their own issues. In other words they have their own devils to fight. The empathy perspective will redirect how you deal with the scarred ones. How you respond to somebody else's hurt that has caused them to become bitter and difficult will be vital to their deliverance. Let's look at some scripture.

1: Corinthians 13:7 in the English Standard Version

"7: Love bears all things, believes all things, hopes all things, endures all things."

Love Bears All Things:

I am going to tolerate what's making me uncomfortable because of love.

Love Believes All Things

I've got the faith to believe that your process will not be your outcome.

Love Hopes All Things

I have a desire to see you survive and walk to your expected end.

Love Endures All Things

No matter how long it takes, I am here with you till the end.

Do You Have the Capacity

The capacity is the maximum amount that something can contain: Do you have what it takes to love the broken and the wounded. Anytime I am exposed to somebodies' brokenness it is clear that this is my assignment which means I have been assigned to that person by God. I have the tools that's needed to be effective, I just have to put it into practice. I must exercise patience with the patients because how I handle them is being evaluated through a divine lens.

Galatians 6:2

"2: Bear ye one another's burdens, and so fulfill the law of Christ."

You must approach this chosen assignment with the mindset that I am called to help you carry your burden. It is too heavy for you to do it alone, so I am here to help you with the process. Whatever you do, always continue to sharpen your focus when dealing with the scars.

What is my focus point? Why am I here? God brought me to it to see you through it. No, I am not God, but he sent me to you to assist you because God has plans for you, and when I participate in helping the broken to reach the breakthrough phase of life, I have just been a part of a destiny turn, but satan's job is to not just attack you but also attack the assistant which is your support group. He wants your support to grow weary also, but we stand on:

Galatians 6:9 - King James Version

"9: And let us not be weary in well doing: for in due season we shall reap if we faint not."

Discerning The Isolation of the Scarred

While you are interacting with the scarred believer, you must watch out for isolation. One of the things that the enemy of our soul loves to do is isolate the broken from love. Yes, he wants to influence them that nobody cares, and disgruntlement and bitterness and guilt start to drive them into the chamber of despair, but you, the one that's called and assigned to this fight, must watch, fight, and pray and look for the signs of isolation. When the scarred are trying to separate themselves, you must be intentional in your fellowship with them. It will not only keep them driving toward the goal, but it will also keep them accountable.

The Grace to Cover Me and Carry Me

When I say God has assigned me to you and I got the capacity of love for you. I'm actually saying to you scarred believer that I can cover you. Your heart is safe with me: I will not reveal what is concealed because remember while I'm on this assignment I am being evaluated through a divine lens.

Chapter 6 – Dealing With A Wounded Spirit

In this chapter, I want to address a present problem that affects us all. Whether you are saved or not, in church or out of church, on the executive board at the city's finest organization, none of us are exempt from life's unexpected twists and turns, and there is a storm that can wreck your life without invitation and in the aftermath leaving you brokenhearted and oppressed in spirit. These are scars, not just any scar, but a mark that's engraved deep in the soul.

Reminder

"Some people have scars on them while others have scars in them."

Proverbs 18:14 - King James Version

"14: The spirit of a man will sustain his infirmity; but a wounded spirit who can bear?"

What Does It Mean to Have a Wounded Spirit?

A wounded spirit refers to injury to the <u>unseen areas</u> of our being, including mind, emotions, and will.

The word translated means to be broken or crushed.

As I studied this topic, I have concluded that many in our society struggle with being a victim of a wounded spirit. Whether it's in your family, in your neighborhood, on your secular job, or even in the church, we find people from all different walks of life carrying around a wounded spirit. No one wakes up and says to themselves, "This is a good day to become a drug addict or a potential alcoholic." Sometimes, LIFE happens, and the results of your outcome depend on how you respond to the crisis. How do you cope with the pain after a loss, being betrayed by a close friend, or even trying to cope with the reality of going through a divorce when you made a vow that no matter what, we are supposed to stay together? A wounded spirit, according to biblical scriptures, says that a wounded person is hard to bear, but our God is able to do all things to those who believe.

There Is a War in the Unseen Area

As discussed earlier that a wounded spirit refers to injury to the unseen areas. Dealing with scarred people we realize that often you may experience them having manifestations of an inside fight. It's a soul scar, you can't see it but it's there and its wounded them.

The Enemy Comes Only To Steal, Kill and Destroy

(Ephesians 6:12)

"<u>For we do not wrestle against flesh and blood</u>, but against the rulers, against the authorities, against the cosmic powers over this present darkness, against the spiritual forces of evil in the heavenly places."

Dealing with a generation suffering from wounded spirit is not physical fight, but a spiritual fight that must be handled with the right tact and strategy.

What are Considered Unseen Injuries?

These are the scars that we carry with us from generation to generation, like living, breathing trauma that won't go away. They impact you progressively, and these internal scars manifest and reveal non-productive fruit that will occur without physical signs. Think about the countless stories of the Pastor shepherding over a large multicultural church, and the ministry seemed to be thriving, one Sunday, the man of God stood flat-footed behind the sacred desk of the pulpit and declared God's word with power, passion, and holy conviction. Lives were saved, deliverance manifested all through the sanctuary, joy was flowing, restoration and transformation were happening that day, and just he greeted the people in his benediction and left with what appeared to be happiness written all over him and went home, locked himself in his office, wrote his last letter to his family and committed suicide. How could this be? How could this happen to God's man? Could it be that the Pastor was suffering from a wounded spirit or trauma that was unchecked and left him with a wound:

an injury in an unseen place? Another name for these are hidden wounds. These wounds can cause a cycle in the mind that is very consistent at recalling pain on every level. These inside wounds give birth to insecurities, frustration, and deep-rooted anger. Those of you who are reading this particular book, let us get honest with ourselves: can you recognize and expose at least one hidden wound in your life? If so, I believe it's time to break the cycle.

"The Wounds We Don't Unmask Will Become My Personal Prison"

Overcoming Rejection That Leaves a Scar

I have come to understand some things by way of endowed knowledge and also by experience. Rejection is a real thing, and it will crush and leave you paralyzed. It attacks your self-esteem and oftentimes persuades you to settle in areas where you wouldn't have settled. Rejection has the ability to taint a person's decisions. It brings me through a moment of self-pity and isolation, and if I'm not careful, I will develop the mindset of a victim. The sense of not being wanted, abandoned, and stereotyped can leave your spirit wounded.

Rejection means to cast aside, to throw away, to put aside.

Psalm 27:10

"10: When my father and my mother forsake me, then the Lord will take me up."

Overcoming Rejection and Exposing the Enemy

Rejection creates demonic bondage by bringing you to a place of isolation. Now, let's look at this concept because when satan isolates us, he does so to assassinate to eliminate, but when God brings you to and through isolation, it brings about revelation. We see it in scripture when Elijah slew all the false prophets of Baal on Mount Carmel and Jezebel threatened his life. He ran into where he met God, and he instructed and led him to a cave for his isolation, and there we find God was really positioning him to unlock this next level.

The fruit of rejection

Rejection causes emotional wounds, which, if not purified and let go, will grow and multiply into unhealthy fruit. These spiritual wounds will open you up to evil spirits, leaving you vulnerable to the enemy's attack.

Let's Have a Conversation About This Fruit

Seeking man's approval on life decisions because of insecurity.

Basing your identity on the perception of others.

Envy and jealousy are fruits of rejection.

Fear of confrontation (because your identity is based upon what they think of you).

Struggling with Constructive Criticism.

Stubbornness is rooted in rejection.

Rejection Strips a person of Love and Acceptance.

Another fruit from which to guard your heart is the Spirit of Resentment, which is an extension of rejection.

There is a scarred generation of people suffering from a wounded spirit, BUT!

BUT THERE IS GOOD NEWS!

Jesus Had a Mission to Heal the Brokenhearted

When Christ walked the earth, a vital part of his ministry focused on the brokenhearted suffering with wounded spirits. As we follow his methodological strategy for dealing with the multitudes, we notice clearly that before he preached any sermon, taught any lesson, or communicated any parable, the bible says that he had compassion on them. As a matter of fact, in the Gospel of Matthew 9:35-37, we find these words written:

"35: And Jesus went about all the cities and villages, teaching in their synagogues, and preaching the gospel of the kingdom, and healing every sickness and every disease among the people.

36: But when he saw the multitudes, he was moved with compassion on them because they fainted and were scattered abroad, as sheep having no shepherd."

He ushered in a deliverance that the people could see. He brought a movement that was life-changing, and what our world needs is vessels that are submitted to God, who packs and carries an anointing that touches the soul of a man. Demons were cast out, forgiveness was being rendered, and restoration began to spread like wildfire. This anointing was tailor-made for the outcast, downtrodden, and those who were suffering with a wounded spirit being broken and crushed by the trials of life. There was no hope for those consumed by the darkness.

We come to understand that somebody who is suffering from a wounded spirit is dealing with weight in their inner man. It's a heaviness that is progressively breaking down to the point of exhaustion and fatigue, and the atmosphere of despair is closing in on them.

My prayer to God is when I operate in the field, and I interact with people help me Lord to discern their heaviness.

"Let's Deal With The Heaviness"

When there is heaviness on the inside, nothing outside seems clear. This heaviness drains you emotionally and robs you spiritually. This heaviness has the characteristics of a thief who watches and observes and slithers in and surrounds me internally to the point of depression. I want to lift my hands, but I'm struggling right now, and I desperately need a breakthrough because this wounded spirit is driving me. I heard somewhere in the good book that according to:

Isaiah 61:3

"3: To appoint unto them that mourn in Zion, to give unto them beauty for ashes, the oil of joy for mourning, the garment of praise for the spirit of heaviness; that they might be called trees of righteousness, the planting of the Lord, that he might be glorified."

In context, we must come to know that in this scripture we have three tools to use and one declaration.

1. Beauty for Ashes
2. Oil of Joy for Mourning
3. The Garment of Praise for the Spirit of Heaviness

The Declaration of Gods Promise

that they might be called trees of righteousness, the planting of the Lord, that he might be glorified.

God has a Strategy for those Dealing With a Wounded Spirit

Beauty For Ashes

I am going to adorn you with beauty when you should be putting on ashes.

Oil of Joy for Mourning

I'm going to birthed in you a triumph on the inside in spite of the circumstances on the outside.

The Garment of Praise for the Spirit of Heaviness

I'm going to clothe you with thanksgiving that creates a sound that will lift up a standard against the spirit of heaviness.

"See you in the chapter as we discuss unveiling the root of bitterness"

Chapter 7 – Unveiling The Root Of Bitterness

In this chapter, we will address the root of bitterness that sometimes-scarred people have to deal with, which is that scars impact our lives in more ways than one. Have you ever had bitterness to dominate your life and taint the heart? In Proverbs 4:23 in the New International Version, it tells us that:

"23: Above all else, guard your heart, for everything you do flows from it."

Once bitterness gets in the heart it disrupts peace and stills your joy producing what I call unnecessary noise of the mind that dismantles your thought process and holds you captive.

Scripture: Hebrews 12:15

"15: See to it that no one falls short of the grace of God and that no bitter root grows up to cause trouble and defile many,

Sharpness of taste; lack of sweetness,

A state of mind that is a mix of anger, sadness, and disappointment"

PikrÃ-a (bitterness), it conveys an extremely bitter, harsh, and distasteful condition.

In The Hebrew Context

Leader מ - ר - ר Verb – (archaic); to make someone's life miserable (archaic).

In The Greek Context

Literally or figuratively:--bitterness means poison.

Please, Somebody Help Me; I'm a Carrier of Poison

In Hebrew culture, any poisonous plant is called a "bitter" plant. Poison kills, and the result of ingesting a poison would be life-threatening. When you are consumed with bitterness, it taints your vision and shatters your view. Imagine the people today viewing life from the lens of bitterness. Everything you see is negative, and you refuse to embrace a life of peace because something is missing, and your bitterness is deeply rooted the more you practice bitterness. The harsh reality is the beloved, the carrier of the poison, is normally the one who ends up suffering. This poison of bitterness will dismantle you inside out. Bitter people reject Godly fellowship because it is this type of atmosphere that refreshes, encourages, and motivates us. When you are in a season of trials, you need to guard yourself and pray intentionally because Satan thrives off of us becoming bitter in the trial. Rather, God desires for us to become better in the trial by honoring him giving God the glory and rendering thanksgiving.

What is the root of bitterness, and how can it defile many?

Through observation, we notice that the root of bitterness doesn't just affect the embittered individual, but it contaminates and affects everyone you are connected to or in a relationship with. It affects their whole outlook on life, tormenting them with vexation of spirit because they are bitter, and they will defile anyone outside of their bitterness. Let's look at a mother who is raising three girls on her own and is still struggling with the concept of an absent father in her life. She is hurt, disappointed, angry, and later becomes resentful of the situation; if she is not careful, she will become bitter, and as a result, she starts to lash out at the children, addressing them from a negative place and releasing damaging words that can leave a child traumatized and hurt and at least one of them out the sibling group becomes bitter on how they were raised with a contentious mother, and now they too develop bitterness, and so now the root of bitterness has now become a generational shackle that's got to be addressed and broken because bitterness if not handled become contagious so it can start with person but it has the ability to defile many.

"A Bitter Root Will Bear Bitter Fruit"

Matthew 7:15-20

You Will Know Them by Their Fruits

"17: Even so, every good tree bears good fruit, but a bad tree bears bad fruit. 18: A good tree cannot bear bad fruit, nor can a bad tree bear good fruit. 19: Every tree that does not bear good fruit is cut down and thrown into the fire. 20: Therefore, by their fruits, you will know them."

Fruits of Bitterness

- Bitterness reflects resentment, and it fuels a perpetual grudge.
- An Unwillingness to Forgive.
- Bitterness lacks grace and kindness.
- Bitterness conceals resentment and keeps a record of wrongs.
- Bitterness is a supporter of extended animosity.
- Bitterness corrupts my conversations.
- Bitterness refuses and rejects reconciliation.

Bitterness In Relationships

In relationships, there are many times that if you watch closely, you will notice bitterness in your partner. What do you do when your partner starts to grow bitter towards you and it is almost like it's impossible to deal with them at that point? As it relates to loving people with scars, is it possible that you may have a scar or hidden wound that according to their perspective may be caused by yourself?

One of the challenges of being in a relationship with a bitter person is we must recognize the cycle of bitterness as it comes. Bitterness is hard on relationship and if it is not dealt with accordingly, it can cause a wedge that will divide.

The key to dealing with the root of bitterness in a person is that if you love them, you must have what I call intentional love. Your patience must be relentless as well as consistent. I believe one of the greatest challenges in relationships is to suffer with a bitter person because, remember, its poison to the one who is concealing it, and you have to prepare yourself for the process. There is always a why behind everything. This simply means you have to stop and ask yourself, what happened? Why is my spouse or significant other person so bitter towards me? It's almost like we are enemies in the same household. This will now bring you through a deep, intense examination.

Bitterness is a toxic emotion that can consume us from the inside out, affecting us mentally, emotionally, and physically. If left unchecked, bitterness can lead to a multitude of other negative emotions like hate, jealousy, and even depression.

To summarize, recognizing the signs of bitterness is essential in addressing this toxic emotion.

As we close this chapter, we say:

Pull It Up By the Roots

When something is rooted deep, it is difficult to disconnect like a tree with deep roots. Those roots have entrenched themselves in the soil and have grown thick and strong. The root of bitterness in our hearts must be uprooted quickly before they mature.

A bitter root will leave a scar on the soul if we delay dealing with it.

In our conclusion of this chapter, reflect on the following:

<u>Ephesians 4:31</u>

"31: Get rid of all bitterness, rage and anger, brawling and slander, along with every form of malice."

Pull It Up By The Roots!

Chapter 8 – I Forgive You, But I'm Still Offended

In my years of ministry as a lay member and my 13 years of Pastoring, I have discovered that two of the most sensitive topics to unravel are the subjects of forgiveness and offense. In any type of relationship, there will be moments when somebody has to forgive somebody, and it is impossible to escape this life without having to experience some type of offense. When you have wronged someone, and it has been brought to your acknowledgment, and you render a sincere, authentic apology, and in your heart, you feel the Godly sorrow that works repentance, but you still sense some residue of anger and resentment manifesting in their behaviors towards you which forces you to draw the conclusion that they say they forgave me, but it appears they are still offended.

Scripture Reference:

Matthew 6:14-15: "For if you forgive others their trespasses, your heavenly Father will also forgive you, but if you do not forgive others their trespasses, neither will your Father forgive."

Colossians 3:13: "Bearing with one another and, if one has a complaint against another, forgiving each other; as the Lord has forgiven you, so you also must forgive."

We must first understand the harsh reality of forgiveness. Forgiveness is a process; sometimes, it is a progressive work and not spontaneous. It can take time for someone to fully release the negative and continue to work through their feelings.

What is forgiveness?

Releasing the offender from guilt and the debt they owe us or letting go.

Forgiveness is a Decision

We know the principles of forgiveness. In a moment where you have been violated, you still struggle emotionally to forgive because this person has scarred you deeply and you know BIBLE, however, you're in a battle. But, at the end of the day the right thing to do is to be intentional in forgiveness because it's a vital part of us perfecting that love walk.

Head Knowledge vs. Heart Posture

In my head I make the decision to forgive because I know, according to the scriptures, it's what I'm supposed to do.

BUT

My heart is really far from the decision that I exercised really good lip service, but my heart was not in accord with my words, so in essence, I said I forgive, but really, I'm still offended, and so, now I must tolerate what I'm uncomfortable with because I'm still OFFENDED.

"Forgiveness is a powerful act of grace, restoration, and healing that impacts the forgiver and the forgiven."

Ephesians 4:32 – "Be kind to one another, tenderhearted, forgiving one another, as God in Christ forgave you."

As we come to understand Fellowship among the believers, we must acknowledge that we are all saved by the blood of the lamb. However, we come from different backgrounds and walks of life, and the truth of the matter is; sometimes as we work to build bonds of unity, we will rub each other, but God has a strategy to deal with the madness. The principles must be worked out to see the results.

I further emphasize the reciprocal nature of forgiveness and how it benefits us to practice this principle, because when we do open ourselves up to receive God's forgiveness.

What are the benefits of forgiving someone?

You release yourself from being put in a position to harbor resentment and bitterness, which could lead to emotional, spiritual, and physical bondage.

Forgiveness That Produces Reconciliation

- First, recognize that Reconciliation is a process.
- The process of Reconciliation depends on the attitude of the offender (are you sincere).
- Accepts full responsibility for his or her actions.
  - Welcomes and embraces accountability.
  - Be honest about your motives.
  - Be humble in your attitude.

Let's point out and discuss three reasons why people with scars struggle with forgiveness:

Reason #1: Unhealed Emotions

- After forgiveness comes the healing of the emotions.
- Working through the pain of the offense and learning how to process it.

Reason #2: It's still happening

- Consistent behavior that breached built-up trust.
- There is a remaining cycle of repeated mistakes.
- Refuse to embrace the accountability process.

Reason #3: You haven't accepted the reality

- Forgiveness releases the offender; it doesn't change them.
- False expectations will set you up for future disappointments.
- Changes are made where there are adjustments.

Forgiveness is a Command

God's requirement to forgive is not merely a suggestion. It's a command.

Colossians 3:13 tells us that as the Lord has forgiven you, you <u>must</u> also forgive.

It must mean to be commanded or requested to do or carry out.

ONCE AGAIN, YOU MUST

Luke 6:37 says, "Forgive, and you will be forgiven.

Matthew 6:15 states, "But if you do not forgive others their trespasses, neither will your Father forgive your trespasses."

Why Am I Still Offended?

"17: Then said he unto the disciples, it is impossible, but that offense will come: but woe unto him, through whom they come!

2: It was better for him that a millstone was hanged about his neck and he cast into the sea than that he should offend one of these little ones.

3: Take heed to yourselves: If thy brother trespass against thee, rebuke him; and if he repent, forgive him.

4: And if he trespasses against thee seven times in a day, and seven times in a day turn again to thee, saying, I repent; thou shalt forgive him.

5: And the apostles said unto the Lord, increase our faith."

The Offense

A stumbling block or cause of temptation (Isaiah 8:14; Matthew 16:23; 18:7). Greek skandalon, properly that at which one stumbles or takes offense.

A cause of transgression or wrong.

The Offended

Feeling or expressing hurt, indignation, or irritation because of a perceived wrong.

The thief cometh not but to steal, kill, and destroy.

Jesus says the thief comes to do three things: steal, kill, and destroy.

Steal is the **Greek word klepto**. It means to remove something secretly or stealthily.

Kill is the **Greek word to**. It means to slay, usually with the purpose of offering a sacrifice.

Destroy is the **Greek word Apollo.** It means to put an end to something, to ruin, to kill.

Understanding The Wiles of The Devil

As we continue to discuss the scars that people carry, Satan plays on the vulnerability of people who are suffering with whatever level of soul wounds you are dealing with.

Wiles are tricks or manipulations designed to deceive someone. Wiles of the devil are clever schemes used by Satan to ensnare and trap us. Through a wounded experience he battle against the mind attempting to give birth to unfruitful thoughts and the design is to influence to entertain the thoughts and allow them to take root until I am now rooted deep in bitterness and walking in offense and now I have become bitter but God has given us a counterattack.

Ephesians 6:11

Warns us to "put on the whole armor of God that ye may be able to stand against the wiles of the devil."

Satan is very crafty in his approach; he attacks us during crises and wounded moments.

To combat the wiles of the devil, we must at all times stay clothed with the armor of God.

We must stay ready to keep from getting ready.

Armor Of God
Ephesians 6:10

The Helmet Of Salvation

The Breastplate Of Righteousness

The Shield Of Faith

The Belt Of Truth

The Sword Of The Spirit

Feet Prepared With Gospel Of Peace

Discerning the Trap of the Enemy

They use offense as a trap to confine us to our own thoughts, which have been compromised because of the offense.

<u>If you have ever been offended, you know how it felt.</u>

In the church, the offense is a huge stumbling block to the salvation of the lost.

Skándalon – properly, the trigger of a trap (the mechanism closing a trap down on the unsuspecting victim);

Offense has broken up many and dismantled many church organizations and caused division in the body of Christ.

Satan's Trap

When we are offended, we tend to shut down and isolate ourselves from the other person, and as long as we are absent from their presence, we feel that the offense has been released, but the minute we are in the perimeters of their presence, we feel triggers that send us to recall of the hurt all over again and in turn, the offense is rewatched because I said I forgave them and I was done with it but the harsh reality is, I am still OFFENDED which the trap of the enemy to <u>keep me bound by my own mind.</u>

Let's Take a Look At The Fruit

The Fruit of Offense

- Hurt
- Anger
- Outrage
- Jealousy

- Envy
- Resentment
- Strife
- Bitterness
- Hatred

Conflict Resolution

Matthew 18:15-17 (NLT)

If another believer sins against you, go privately and point out the offense. If the other person listens and confesses it, you have won that person back. But if you are unsuccessful, take one or two others with you and go back again so that everything you say may be confirmed by two or three witnesses. If the person still refuses to listen, take your case to the church. Then if he or she won't accept the church's decision, treat that person as a pagan or a corrupt tax collector.

Humility Serves

In Mark 10:35–45, we see the realities of offense even attacks the inner circle of Jesus, you see nobody is exempt from the spirit of offense.

James and John asked Jesus for power and position.

"Grant us to sit, one at your right hand and one at your left, in your glory."

As those close to Jesus, the brothers felt they deserved places of honor next to the Lord. But it gets worse: "And when the ten heard it, they began to be indignant at James and John."

Jesus's Response

(Mark 10:43–45)

"But whoever would be great among you must be your servant, and whoever would be first among you must be slave of all. For even the Son of Man came not to be served but to serve, and to give his life as a ransom for many."

In Our Summary, We Conclude:

Ask yourself, is it possible that because of wounded a experience, I exercised forgiveness with the lips but the truth is, I'm still offended?

Don't give in.

Reflect and evaluate the situation.

Recognize it's a trap of the enemy.

Renew your mind.

In closing this chapter, I leave you with this:

2 Corinthians 10:5

"5: Casting down imaginations, and every high thing that exalted itself against the knowledge of God, and bringing into captivity every thought to the obedience of Christ."

Chapter 9 – I Trusted You With My Heart

As we move into the concept of loving people with scars, oftentimes, you may be connected to or in covenant with a person who has suffered a broken heart. Dealing with a broken heart is very difficult, and if that person is not completely healed from this brokenness, you could cause major complications in your relationship. When we love or choose to love, we do it with passion. When I say I love you and want to spend the rest of my life with you, I am not just exchanging vows at the altar, but I'm actually giving the individual my heart, and I am consciously saying I trust you with my heart, it's fragile so please handle this package with caution, and they promise to NEVER HURT you.

The Understanding of Trust

Trust: Is a firm belief in the reliability, truth, ability, or strength of someone or something.

Whether you believe it or not, trust is a big deal. When people gain our trust, it matters. It puts a lot of weight on relationship building.

Trust is an important pillar in relationships, and the lack of it can lead to an unhealthy relationship that produces conflict, insecurity, depression, and division.

Promotes Safety

Trust communicates to you that you are safe with me, and I give you permission to inspect and observe my consistency.

Eliminates Drama & Contention

Trust also allows you to navigate conflict. When you trust your partner, you create an atmosphere that is conducive to peace and tranquility.

Increases Your Bond

Establishing trust creates a strong bond and foundation to build on. Knowing you can trust your partner promotes increased closeness and safety. When you trust one another, you feel safe knowing that your partner has your back and can be relied upon through anything.

Reliability is when someone does what they say they're going to do consistently.

Breaking Trust

Trust is broken in many ways between friends, family, spouses, and children. Each requires different levels of restoration, Reconciliation, and willingness from both parties. Someone who has experienced some type of betrayal, such as unfaithfulness in a relationship, may develop trust issues that can interfere with future relationships. Breaking trust is like a breach in the wall. Once the wall is cracked, it is considered damaged property, and the only thing left to do is fix the crack, or it will continue to get bigger and bigger. After forgiveness has been initiated in a breach or broken trust, you must understand and embrace the process. You now must be patient with the rebuilding process of rebuilding that trust again. When you trust somebody with your heart, and they hurt you, that trust has been broken, and there is a question that is asked psychologically, and that is, can I trust you with my heart again? Because we must know that love is a risk? The person you are giving your heart to may not live up to your expectations, and when that is manifested, it makes it difficult to trust that person again.

Rebuilding Trust

Trust in an intimate relationship is rooted in feeling safe with another person. Infidelity, lies, or broken promises can damage the trust connection between partners, that will produce trust issues. The key to rebuilding is understanding, first; it takes time and consistent work effort to re-establish the sense of safety you need for a relationship to thrive and continue to grow. Recovery from broken trust will not be able work without accountability.

Understanding The Heart

The heart is a powerful force that drives our actions and influences our thinking and behavior.

Proverbs 4:23 says, "Above all else, guard your heart, for everything you do flows from it."

What Does it Mean to "Guard Your Heart?"

When there is a breach of trust in a relationship, it forces your partner to guard your heart. Our heart is the source of our thoughts, attitudes, beliefs, and actions. Therefore, it is crucial to guard our hearts above all else. Guarding our hearts is about protecting ourselves from future hurt. It is imperative to find a balance between guarding your heart and allowing trust to flow freely. What's important is your response after trust has been broken. You have a choice in how you respond, but whatever, you do don't operate in victimization. Victimization is characterized by an attitude of powerlessness, blaming others for the negative situations in your life.

Now, Let's Put It All Together

Trust + Heart

- **Trust: firm belief in the reliability, truth, ability, or strength of someone or something.**

- **Heart: the central or innermost part of something.**

- **A belief that my partner is reliable enough and has the ability to be given the opportunity to handle the core of me which is my heart.**

Let's Start Peeling Away Some Layers

What's a Covenant?

A covenant is a relationship between two partners who make binding promises to each other and work together to reach a common goal. They're often accompanied by oaths, signs, and ceremonies. Covenants define obligations and commitments as we reflect on marriage. The husband and wife choose to enter into a formal relationship, binding themselves to one another in lifelong faithfulness and devotion.

Broken Vows: We Was Supposed to Stay Together

What happens when those vows are broken? Me having been in a marriage for 13 years, which ended in divorce, I must confess I was a bit bitter about the breakup at first because I always had the mindset and the expectation that no matter what, we were supposed to stay together. The worst part of a relationship is when your partner makes the bold statement that I'm not happy, and I don't love you anymore, and you must love me enough to let me go. This type of expression can occasionally bring you through a sense of rejection. So now you are torn between staying in a marriage where your spouse claims she or he doesn't love you anymore or giving in to the reality of divorce.

Let me be clear: Marriage covenants are meant to be permanent, and a lack of working healthy marriage principles is always to blame when a marriage ends in divorce. We commit sin when we break our vows, and marriage requires the regular practice of confession and forgiveness for the failures and oversights between spouses.

The sin in divorce lies in the breaking of marriage vows, not necessarily in the divorce itself. God's own divorce was entirely due to Israel's hardhearted sin. God was the blameless victim of divorce. When God says, "I hate divorce" **(Mal. 2:16),** he says so not with the furious pointed finger of a judge, but with the brokenheartedness of one who has experienced the devastation of rejection and betrayal at the hands of his beloved.

"God Wants Heal You Everywhere You Hurt"

Chapter 10 – I'm Waiting on My Physician

As we go into this chapter, we have set before us one of the most valuable key elements to dealing with or loving people who are suffering from scars, and that is the discipline of waiting. This idea came with a real statement and a real story. As previously discussed in chapter three, the Pastor and wife, who were both suffering from their own personal addictions and having a heated discourse over her addictions his wife make a statement when she assumes through his body language that he was attempting to call it quits, that she says to him with tears rolling down her cheeks, "I'm waiting on my physician."

This is one of the most powerful statements I have ever heard as it relates to waiting on a solution to a problem. This is a person who knows that they are in a process but is very confident that, at some point, they will experience the end of this process and embrace her breakthrough.

Surviving The Waiting Room

The Bible's perspective on waiting involves trusting the source of why you are there. I must admit there have been times when I went to the waiting room, and because the physician could not see me promptly, I left the waiting room without getting a solution to my problem. Maybe I was not hurting bad enough because when the pain hits you just right, you will have to take some patience pills, weather the storm, and see it to the end.

Patience says we are faithfully trusting and standing in position until our physician shows up. It's just like waiting on God for a miracle. Job said, "I will wait until my change comes."

To wait means to be aware of all of your feelings about what is happening around you and to discern the right time to do the next thing.

One reason waiting, in general, is problematic is that we live in a fast-paced culture and society that constantly promotes the pursuit of instant gratification. No one wants to have to wait for anything. We want spontaneous results right away, and we struggle to embrace any process requiring time and patience. We want things to happen in our time and according to our plans.

We even have that demanding and impatient attitude as Christians. When something is beyond our own understanding and forces us to wait on God for answers to our prayers, that can translate into delayed vision, unreached life goals, and not having a need or desire met, and in turn, we become frustrated in the waiting room.

Psalm 33:20

"Our soul waits for the Lord; He is our help and our shield."

We not only wait, but we wait patiently, and when this principle is worked, we open ourselves up to change.

As Isaiah 40:31 says, "…those who wait on the Lord shall renew their strength…"

Kingdom Thought

We don't get what we deserve, we get what we expect and sometimes the value of wholeness comes with a price and its called waiting!

Scripture References On Waiting

Psalm 27:14

"Wait on the Lord; be of good courage, and He shall strengthen your heart; wait, I say, on the Lord!"

James 5:7-8

"Therefore, be patient, brethren, until the coming of the Lord. See how the farmer waits for the precious fruit of the earth, waiting patiently for it until it receives the early and latter rain. You also be patient. Establish your hearts, for the coming of the Lord is at hand."

Being patient in the seasons of pruning, waiting, and growth, because every season is purposeful and understand that his timing is perfect. That wife of the

Pastor who was waiting on the physician was willing to embrace her process with confidence by stating that her physician will show up.

Discerning Your Symptoms

When your name is called and they take your vitals and everything is checked out, the nurse examines the patient and says, "What are your symptoms?"

That was always peculiar to me, that I have to assess my own pain and explain the complications. And the nurse documents your response and then he or she reports the information to the physician.

The Diagnosis

Diagnosis is the identification of the nature and cause of a certain phenomenon or the process of determining the nature of a problem. When doing a proper study on people who are living with spiritual scars and wounded spirits, you will come to find out that the scars are the evidence that that person has experienced something that caused a scar, but however, the diagnosis is designed to reveal the nature or the origin of the problem. Every time a counselor sees a patient, one of their first orders of business is to get them to trust the process that's in place and to open up and TALK ABOUT IT because in doing so, they are literally letting you into their life by telling the story and the counselor's job at this point is to listen. When we listen to the hearts of scarred people, then we can determine a proper diagnosis that is deeper than the behaviors that we see. One counselor after listening to the story of a client who was addicted to drugs, the counselor made a solid diagnosis and told the client, "Based on what I've heard so far, you don't have a drug problem; you have a traumatization problem. You need to be healed of the hurt that you are carrying. You must heal before you will ever be able to walk into recovery."

"REMEMBER, SOME PEOPLE HAVE SCARS ON THEM WHILE OTHERS HAVE SCARS IN THEM"

"Now that the diagnosis has been made, it is time to see the physician."

Jesus, The Great Physician

Matthew 11:28-29

"28: Come unto me, all ye that labor and are heavily laden, and I will give you rest.

29: Take my yoke upon you, and learn of me; for I am meek and lowly in heart: and ye shall find rest unto your souls."

Jesus is often referred to as "The Great Physician". In older saints or Christians, they would say he is a doctor in a sick room. When we read and study the Four Gospels of Jesus Christ according to Mathew, Mark, Luke, and John, we discover he performed many diverse miracles during His ministry on earth.

(Mark 2:17 KJV)

"When Jesus heard it, he saith unto them, they that are whole have no need of the physician, but they that are sick: I came not to call the righteous, but sinners to repentance."

The God of all Grace Came Just For Your Diagnosis

Let's Look at Jesus' Resume

- Healed the blind (Matthew 9:27-31).
- Healed the deaf and mute (Mark 7:31-37).
- Healed the lame (John 5:5-9).
- Cleansed the leper (Mark 1:40-44).
- Dealt with demon possession (Luke 4:31-37).
- Raised the dead (John 11:38-44).

In Summary

"When Jesus Walks Into Your Room, Everything Changes"

Chapter 11 – The Benediction: A Word for The Scarred

From the Author

Blessings, family, friends, and beloved. My prayer is that this book touched you in places that you have not been touched before. Being a person growing up in a challenged childhood has had my share of physical, spiritual, and hidden scars. I was one of the ones who walked around with scars on them, and I suppressed them by succumbing to drugs and gang affiliation. The reality is that I had unchecked trauma that I had not dealt with, so the result is that my trauma grew with me until later in my adulthood. My spouse at the time challenged me to go see a counselor because what I needed was a HEALTHY CONFRONTATION to deal with the little boy inside of me that had never been healed. My purpose was to minister to your soul where you can, too, be on the road to spiritual recovery.

Remember, beloved family:

"GOD WANTS TO HEAL YOU EVERYWHERE YOU HURT "

About the Author

Overseer/Pastor James G. Savoy

He is God's Man of Faith and Influence, one who is sent by God to impact the world with a Prophetic-EmoweringMessage of Healing, Deliverance, and Restoration for the 21st Century Christian Culture and

Embracing the challenge to reach, restore, and mentor a hurting generation.

Many have been saved, healed, and delivered through his ministry. God has changed many lives through this humble servant throughout the Gospel Field. He is a Servant to the People and a Pastor after God's own heart. Overseer J.G. Savoy is mostly known for his burden to win souls and unique love
for God's people and for challenging the people of God to Tap Into Their Purpose and walk into the Gifting of God.

In 2009, Overseer Savoy heeded the voice of God. By faith, he established a Ministry of Restoration.

The vision was and still is clear: to evangelize the lost, bring

RESTORATION to the brokenhearted and wounded,

and to equip the believers with the power to impact

the nations, To Replace the Misplaced.

Throughout his ministerial journey, he also established

NO Soul Left Behind Outreach Crusades.

Overseer Savoy has made the bold announcement that

God has Favored and bestowed upon me such a great

the privilege of speaking life and building up his people

unto Christ, so I will dedicate and commit my life to the

Gospel of Jesus Christ, Our Lord and Savior!

Milton Keynes UK
Ingram Content Group UK Ltd.
UKHW030944261124
451585UK00001B/256